INTRODUCTION
to
COUNTERPOINT

INTRODUCTION
TO
COUNTERPOINT

by

R. O. MORRIS

LONDON
OXFORD UNIVERSITY PRESS
New York   Toronto

Oxford University Press, Ely House, London W.1

GLASGOW NEW YORK TORONTO MELBOURNE WELLINGTON
CAPE TOWN IBADAN NAIROBI DAR ES SALAAM LUSAKA ADDIS ABABA
DELHI BOMBAY CALCUTTA MADRAS KARACHI LAHORE DACCA
KUALA LUMPUR SINGAPORE HONG KONG TOKYO

ISBN 0 19 317309 3

First edition **1944**
Tenth impression 1975

Printed in Great Britain

CONTENTS

INTRODUCTION

Two great schools of counterpoint have so far evolved in the course of musical history. The first reached its culminating point in the sixteenth century, and Palestrina is generally admitted to be its most authoritative exponent. The other started in the seventeenth century and came to full maturity in the eighteenth, with J. S. Bach—again by common consent—as its supreme master.

The study of counterpoint, as usually taught, begins with a course of 'strict' counterpoint, whose rules claim to embody the principles that guided Palestrina and his contemporaries. Unfortunately this claim is completely bogus. Nobody who knows the A.B.C. of Palestrina's technique can take it seriously for a moment. If 'strict' counterpoint really aspired to do what it professes to do, its rules would have to be entirely reformulated. And this, in competent hands, would be quite a feasible task.

None the less, in my judgment (formed by extensive experience in teaching this subject), the study of counterpoint should not begin with the earlier school, but with the later. Sixteenth-century music, with all its beauty, is apt to sound remote and strange to the beginner when he first makes its acquaintance. Its rhythm and its modality perplex him, while its harmony seems artificially restrained and austere until he has acquired the experience and understanding necessary for its appreciation. The other school, representing the contrapuntal practice not only of Bach and Handel, but also of the great Viennese composers from Haydn to Brahms, strikes a familiar note at once and brings him into immediate contact with a type of music that he already knows and loves. It is this kind of counterpoint that forms the subject-matter of the present volume.

The method followed, however, is basically that of the 'strict' practitioners. Its guiding principle might be described briefly as 'one thing at a time'; that is to say, the student is given a fixed part in plain notes to start with, and then set to work to master various types of movement—two notes to one, four notes to one, suspensions, and so forth—before he embarks on anything approaching a free or variegated rhythm. This is not the only possible way of approaching the subject. But it is a sound method and a tested method; and though it is also a laborious method, it is probably the safest one for the elementary student of average capacity, for whom this book is intended. Therefore, when he finds reference (as he will here and there) to the terminology of 'strict' counterpoint such as 'third' or 'fifth' species, he should relate the description merely to a particular note-pattern—three notes to one, four notes to one, or whatever it may be—and not to the detailed rules and regulations set forth in the 'strict' manuals.

So much for the point of view. There are certain other matters on which a preliminary word of explanation is advisable.

1. Harmony

It is assumed that the student has a knowledge of elementary harmony up to and including the chord of the dominant seventh, passing and other unessential notes, and the rudiments of modulation. I do not think the study of counterpoint—at any rate of this form of counterpoint, which is essentially a process of harmonic decoration—can usefully be started until harmony has been so far learnt.

It is also assumed that the further study of harmony will continue *pari passu* with that of counterpoint, so that by the time the student is half-way or so through this book, he will have a complete outline of harmonic knowledge within the limits of what, for want of a better term, we may call classical music.

2. Compass

I do not think it necessary that early exercises in this form of counterpoint (unlike that of the sixteenth century) should be regarded either as specifically vocal or specifically instrumental in character, at any rate for the first few chapters. Instruments, of course, are more agile than voices, and have a more extended compass. But the first essential for vocal and instrumental counterpoint alike is to acquire a precise, orderly and compact style of writing, and the rules and recommendations made in this book are intended to assist in the formation of such a style, irrespective of medium.

3. Clefs

It is most desirable for the student to become familiar with the alto and the tenor and even the soprano clef as well as the ordinary treble and bass. The fact remains, however, that in most cases he will not be familiar with them when he begins to study counterpoint. Had these clefs, therefore, been used in the illustrations throughout the book, the difficulty of his task would have been increased by the problem of deciphering. And so, not wishing to add to his yoke, I have, rather reluctantly, abstained from the use of the C clefs except in the illustrations to the final chapter. By then he should have become conversant with them, for it is assumed that his teacher will insist on his beginning to use them right from the very start of his contrapuntal studies, otherwise he will never master them

4. *Canti Fermi*

In conclusion, a few remarks about the use of the canti fermi may be helpful. These, with the exception of a few specially designed at the end of chapter v, have been grouped together at the end of the book for the sake of convenience. Set A are plain canti fermi, of short or moderate length, designed for general use with each and every species. Set B are somewhat more extended, more articulate in construction, and in the nature of what are commonly called tunes. These are intended specifically for imitative treatment in three and four parts, as indicated in chapters x, xi, and xii. Set C are no longer in plain notes, but in free rhythm. They have not been designed for imitative treatment, but merely for the addition of two and three similar parts in contrasted but flowing rhythm. At the same time, a certain amount of imitation and interplay between the parts may well be found feasible here and there.

In the first set, at any rate, no C.F. need be regarded as sacrosanct. The beginner must be given something to start on, otherwise he is helpless; that is why a C.F. is provided. But no C.F. is equally well adapted for every possible position or combination of species. One that lends itself readily to the addition of a part in triplets below, for example, may prove highly refractory towards a combination of second and third species above, and so on. In such circumstances, the alteration of a note here and there in the C.F. may well make all the difference to the ease and flow of the counterpoint, without producing any undue distortion of the C.F. itself. In that case, I should regard a little cooking of the C.F. as a musical act of virtue. The idea that a C.F. should never under any circumstances be tampered with is often a frustration of its whole purpose, which (as already remarked) is to help the beginner by giving him a start.

In particular, when a treble C.F., which very likely neither begins nor ends on the tonic note, is transposed for use as a bass, the alteration of the last note or two for the sake of an authentic cadence is surely preferable to the inconclusive inverted cadence to which one may otherwise be reduced.

Be it repeated that these remarks only apply to the plain canti fermi in Set A. The alteration of some well-known tune to facilitate its treatment in such a form as the chorale-prelude is quite another matter. The canto, in such a case, must be regarded as absolutely and not merely relatively fermo.

Chapter One

NOTE AGAINST NOTE

THE added part, whether above or below the C.F., should have a melodic interest and shapeliness of its own, and the two parts together must form the outline of a coherent harmonic progression. It is recommended that in this species the student should add figures to the completed exercise to show the implied chord progressions. This will help him to keep alive to his harmonic responsibilities, and incidentally practise him in using the figured-bass notation, which every musician ought to know.

The two parts as a whole should lie reasonably close together, and seldom or never, in this species, should the interval between them exceed that of a double octave. Contrary and similar movement should be judiciously blended; only exceptionally should either sort continue uninterruptedly as much as three (or at most four) consecutive notes.

Subjoined are some rules to guide the beginner in his choice of melodic and harmonic intervals. They are intended for reference rather than for memorization.

A. Rules of Melodic Progression

1. Use both conjunct and disjunct movement. The former gives firmness and cohesion, the latter the no less indispensable contrast and variety.

2. The widest skip permissible is that of an octave, and this should be approached and quitted from inside itself.

The same applies to the leap of a minor or diminished seventh, and preferably also to that of a major or minor sixth—e.g.:

The leap of a major seventh is best avoided in this species.

3. There should rarely be more than two successive leaps (and never more than three) in the same direction, and the combined range of these should not exceed the octave:

4. Leaps of an augmented interval are to be avoided, except possibly between the 6th and 7th degrees of the harmonic minor scale. And in such a situation it is preferable (and usually feasible) to use the melodic minor form instead.

5. Skips of a diminished 5th or diminished 7th may be used, provided

they are followed by the note immediately above the lower or the note immediately below the higher note of the interval:

But if the second note of the diminished interval bears a stronger accent than the first, more freedom of action is permissible, e.g.:

6. Chromatic alterations of a note, in this species, should only be used for the purpose of modulation.

7. Only in case of necessity should a note be immediately repeated. Such repetition, moreover. must be made from a strong accent to a weak, not from a weak to a strong, except in case of a sequential formation:

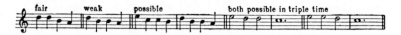

In duple time, the first accent is strong, the second weak. In quadruple time, the first and third are strong, second and fourth weak. In triple time, the second is weak in relation to the first, but strong in relation to the third.

B. Rules of Harmonic Progression

In general, rely largely on the imperfect consonances, using the perfect consonances and the dissonances to give occasional contrast and variety.

In particular, first of all, as regards the consonances:

1. *Unison.* Should be avoided, in this species, except on the first and last notes.

2. *Octave.* Should be used somewhat sparingly. Best if approached and quitted by contrary motion, especially if conjunct. It should only be approached by similar motion in cadential or quasi-cadential places, and then the upper part should move to it by step:

3. *Fourth.* Though theoretically consonant, this interval, in two-part work, is for all practical purposes a dissonance. In this species it should be

avoided except occasionally as an idiomatic intermediary between the 2nd and 6th:

4. *Fifth.* Should be used with great caution, being in fact a dangerous element in two-part counterpoint of this type. It is satisfactory in effect as a rule, if approached in similar motion from a third, if the upper part proceeds downwards by step, as at (a) below; or from a sixth, if the upper part proceeds upward by step at (b); or in contrary motion from a tenth (c); or between an essential seventh and a third (d):

Second, as regards the dissonances:

1. *Second.* Safest for the present to use only that major second which can be regarded as an inversion of the dominant 7th, and should be resolved accordingly:

[but also see (3) above].

2. *Seventh.* As far as the diatonic sevenths are concerned, keep to the dominant 7th only until suspensions have been mastered. Diminished 7ths are not much use in two-part counterpoint, as their natural resolution is inwards to the open fifth, which is apt to sound rather bare in this context. In three parts and upward, however, they can be freely used.

3. *Augmented 4th and Diminished 5th.* There is no objection to using these provided they observe the rule that augmented intervals should resolve outwards by step, diminished ones inward by step:

Here are some specimens to illustrate in practice the various points that have been mentioned in this opening chapter:

NOTE AGAINST NOTE

Chapter Two

TWO NOTES TO ONE

A. *Occasional passing-notes*

Before attempting to use continuous two-to-one movement, it will do the student no harm, as a preliminary exercise, to practise adding passing notes here and there, in suitable places, to some of his workings of the canti fermi in the last chapter. Or (better still) he may re-work some of them with this special end in view, adding passing notes to the C.F. itself where opportunity offers, as well as to his own counterpoint. They will be, naturally, of the intermediate (unaccented) kind, and diatonic only.

In this connection he must remember the old caution that unaccented passing notes may create consecutives, but cannot save them. The following, e.g., would both be out of order, even if a third part were added to complete the harmony:

Such progressions as the following are also undesirable in varying degree:

When passing notes have been added to the C.F., those in the counterpoint should usually come in other places. But there is no harm in doubling passing notes occasionally at the third or sixth in parallel movement. The octave may also be doubled as a note in conjunct and contrary movement.

The following specimen will illustrate these various points:

B. *Continuous Two-to-one-Movement*

In this species, not only unaccented diatonic passing notes may be employed, but also auxiliary notes, subsidiary harmony notes, accented passing and auxiliary notes, whether diatonic or chromatic, and (more sparingly) chromatic unaccented passing notes. Indeed, one should say 'must' rather than 'may', if a fluent and idiomatic type of counterpoint is to be achieved (as it can be) within such strict limitation of movement.

A few words about each of these in turn may be useful:

1. *Auxiliary Notes.* If the lower auxiliary lies a full tone below the main note, it may be raised chromatically at will:

Similar chromatic lowering of the upper auxiliary, however, is not recommended. There is no theoretical reason against doing so, it is just that the effect is less felicitous.

2. *Subsidiary Notes.* These need more care and judgment than one might suppose. They should be avoided, for choice, in successive beats, but some successions of this kind are far less objectionable than others. Illustration will make clear at a glance what might be abstruse and pedantic if one attempted to express it in a verbal formula; of the following, the first three are compact and orderly, the remainder sprawl about in most undesirable fashion:

In the lower part, especially, caution is needed. The third above or below the beat note, and the octave, are alone generally admissible. The fourth and fifth, whether above or below, are apt to create a certain harmonic ambiguity, and are therefore best eschewed, except in the special figures illustrated by (d) and (e) hereunder:

Note, however (in anticipation of ch. iii, B. p. 22) that in the following four-note figures the subsidiaries marked + are entirely free from this ambiguity, and may be so used without hesitation:

3. *Accented passing and auxiliary notes.* Such notes should proceed stepwise to the neighbouring harmony note, normally downwards (a) and (b). The upward resolution is only good if the step involved is one of a semitone (c) and (d), or if the accented dissonance is the major sixth of the scale, in which case it may rise happily to the leading note (e). And 7 passing to 8 is always good in effect if taken by conjunct and contrary motion (f):

It may be added here, in anticipation of ch. viii, that a fifth of which one note is an accented passing note cannot give rise to consecutive fifths. The following is blameless:

4. *Unaccented Chromatic Passing Notes.* When the second of two successive essential notes lies a major second above the first, the intermediate step may be supplied by raising the first note chromatically. This procedure should be used with discretion, and the converse (i.e. flattening the higher note if it is the first of the two) is not recommended, except in case of dire extremity:

5. *Accented Chromatic Passing and Auxiliary Notes.* Accented chromatic passing notes are similar in principle to the above, except that in this case the chromatically altered note comes *on* the beat, and the note immediately preceding it (of which it is the chromatic alteration) may itself be either a passing note (a) or an essential note (b). In (c) and (d), chromatic accented auxiliary notes are employed:[1]

[1] In (d), the note D preceding the C sharp is an unessential note, and it is therefore not strictly correct to describe the C sharp as an auxiliary note. But the description may perhaps be allowed to pass for the sake of convenience.

These accented rising dissonances, however, should only be employed, for the present at any rate, when the C.F. is in the lower part.

There is one other figure which ought to be mentioned:

In this figure, the second and fourth notes are purely ornamental notes which are ignored harmonically. It is only available when the essential notes of the counterpoint are moving downwards by step or in the manner of (c) above; the first and third notes of the figure then double the notes of the C.F. in parallel or alternating movement of the 3rd and 6th above or below. It is such an obviously convenient resource that a warning against the excessive use of it may not be out of place.

Specimens:

As this form of counterpoint, at any rate when the C.F. is the upper part, is not less difficult than the species in 3, 4, and 6 notes which follow it, it is recommended that before working the canti fermi on p. 51, the student should begin by completing the preliminary exercises below. In the first three, suitable intermediate notes should be supplied in the upper part; in the other three, in the lower:

THREE, FOUR, SIX AND EIGHT NOTES TO ONE

A. Three Notes to One

As a rule, the first note of the group will be an essential harmony note. The second and third notes may then be almost any combination of passing, auxiliary, and subsidiary notes, the treatment of which should accord with the principles described in the last chapter.

But the first note may also quite well be an accented passing note, diatonic or chromatic. In this case, as a rule, the second note will be the essential harmony note, whilst the third, once more, may be a passing (a), auxiliary (b), or subsidiary (c) note:

Alternatively, the second note may be another ornamental note a third away from the first, so that the third note of the group (the intervening note) is the true harmony note on which the first resolves:

It is important that the above idiom should be defined with absolute precision. Note therefore the following points:

1. If the first note is ultimately going to resolve downwards, the second note will be a third *below* it, and move *upwards* to the third note (a).

2. If the first note is one of the upward-resolving kind, then the second note will be the third *above* it, and move *downwards* to the third note (b).

3. If the third between the first two notes is a major third, it should be reduced to a minor third by raising the second note chromatically (c). (It will be found that this case only arises when the first note is a downward-passing one.)

Also legitimate (and often very convenient) is this procedure:

Here, it will be seen, the third note is a subsidiary note higher than the principal note. The second note is the note immediately above it, which, though unessential, is freely approached by leap from the first note. It is, in fact, a kind of unaccented appoggiatura. It will be noticed in the example given above that this procedure is equally applicable to 4-note groups.

Recourse may also be had to the expedient of 'changing notes'. It is easier to exemplify these before describing them:

It will be seen that the changing notes (marked ⌐¬) act as a sort of link between two statements of the same essential note, of which they are the upper and lower (or lower and upper) neighbours. These changing notes are both unessential, and are ignored harmonically. If the interval between them would normally be a major third, it is usually best to reduce this to a minor third by raising the lower note chromatically, as in (c) and (d) above. If the third is naturally minor it may be left as it is [see (a) and (b) above] or reduced chromatically to a diminished third [(e) and (f)].

Another variant of these changing notes will be found useful occasionally:

Here it will be seen, the changing notes connect two essential notes of which the second lies a third below the first [(a) above]. They cannot well be used between two essential notes of which the second is a third higher than the other, as in (b) above.

Specimens:

B. Four Notes to One

Here, again, principal, subsidiary, passing and auxiliary notes, both accented and unaccented, may be employed in a still greater variety of pattern. But the principles already expounded will be found in every case to govern the procedure, which it would be wearisome to try to analyse into every possible combination. Any intelligent student will find it quicker and simpler to look carefully at the specimens below, in which many, if not all, of the convenient four-note patterns are exemplified. The first group in the first example, by the way (marked ⌐⌐) in four-note grouping, illustrates the use of the 'changing notes' described on p. 21. The other varieties there given are also available in four-note groups:

Specimens:

THREE, FOUR, SIX AND EIGHT NOTES TO ONE

Once more, before proceeding to work the canti fermi on p. 51, the student should, as a preliminary exercise, complete the groups (three- or four-note groups as the case may be) in the following examples, where the first note only of each group is given:

C. Six and Eight Notes to One

Six notes may be regarded as $2+2+2$ (in simple triple time) or $3+3$ (in compound time). Similarly 8 notes may be regarded as $4+4$. Sufficient guidance has therefore already been provided, and no further instructions are needed. Nevertheless, one or two exercises of each type may well be worked for practice, the canti fermi on p. 51 being used for the purpose.

Chapter Four

TIED NOTES AND SUSPENSIONS

A. Tied Notes

ANY essential beat note,[1] in counterpoint, may be tied over to another note that is not of longer time-value than itself. If this second note is a dissonance, it is called a suspension (see B below); otherwise it is called simply a tied note, and is free to proceed by leap or step anywhere, subject of course to the normal canons of melodic movement laid down in earlier chapters.

Tied notes and suspensions alike, if they occur within the bar, are sometimes indicated by the usual sign ⌢; very often, however, they are shown (less correctly) by lengthening the value of the note that is tied, so that there is the appearance of a syncopation:

Syncopation in the modern sense, however, is quite foreign to the contrapuntal style, and the student must habituate himself to recognize and interpret the above *invariably* as:

And in two-part work, ties or suspensions should never occur in both parts simultaneously.

B. Suspensions

A suspended dissonance, as distinct from a tied note, is not free to move anywhere. Dissonance requires resolution, and the dissonant note has to proceed stepwise (and normally downwards) to the nearest harmony note (a, b, c, below). Upward resolutions are sometimes possible (d), and even necessary (e), but they should only be made by the step of a semitone, and should be confined as a rule to the upper part:

[1] The time signature normally indicates the number and value of the beat-notes by means of its numerator and denominator respectively. But beat-values often have to be subdivided. In $4/4$ time, for example, if there is any considerable amount of semiquaver movement, many intermediate quavers will have to be regarded as beat-notes.

It will be noticed in the above ex. that the resolution may either be effected within the same beat as the dissonance (b), or deferred until the next (weak) beat (a and c). In counterpoint the latter is usually to be preferred, as the dissonance is thereby given more time to make its full effect.

It will also be noticed above that in the upper part the 7 6 and 4 3 suspensions are the best available. The 9 8, admirable in three parts, is not so good in two. In the lower part the 2 3 alone is completely satisfactory; the 4 5 and the 7 8 are both to be avoided:

Apropos of consecutives, it is often laid down in text-books that 'progressions which would be incorrect without suspensions are equally incorrect with them'. This is going too far. It is true, as all would agree, that progressions like the following are inadmissible:

In three parts, however, the second of these, in the form given below, is by no means without sanction in classical usage:

And the effect of consecutive fifths in such a case, is further mitigated if the suspension is given one of the ornamental resolutions explained in the next chapter.

Consider also these:

Here the intervening consonances of the 6th completely obliterate any possible impression of consecutive fifths, and both progressions are lawful, though not wholly satisfactory in two-part writing. Note that when the C.F. rises a fourth or falls a fifth it is often possible to introduce a suspended *essential* seventh (or its inversion) in the added part:

It is of the utmost importance to master thoroughly both the theory and practice of tied and suspended notes. Continuous chains of such progressions, however, though prescribed as an exercise by most text-books, are so laboured and unmusical in their effect (especially in the lower part) that I cannot recommend them. A judicious blend of these with ordinary two-notes-to-one movement is to be preferred. Remember that if the second or fourth note is tied it *must* be an essential note. If it is not tied, of course it may equally well be a passing or auxiliary note.

Specimens:

Chapter Five

SUSPENSIONS (CONTINUED)

A. Delayed and Ornamental Resolutions
B. Combination of Movement in the Added Part with Suspensions in the C.F.

A. Ornamental Resolutions. Below are some of the commonest types, in duple and triple (or compound) time:

The above, for the most part, call for observation rather than comment. Note, however, that where the resolution is delayed by the dip of a third [(a) and (b)], the intervening note is usually raised chromatically if the third is major. In (d) observe that the dip is to the nearest intervening note of the chord implied by the resolution. Also that (e) is merely an amplification of (d), effected by filling in the intervening steps between the ornamental note and the resolution. In (f) the jump is upwards, because the resolution is also upwards.

For practice in these resolutions, precisely the same type of exercises may be written as was recommended at the end of the last chapter, but with delayed instead of direct resolutions, and 3 or 4 notes to one (instead of or as well as 2 notes to one) for the intervening movement.

Specimens:

B. Combination of a moving part with a C.F. in suspensions and tied Notes

Ordinary tied notes present no difficulty, because the tie and the subsequent note do not necessarily call for the same harmony, so that the added part has a comparatively wide freedom of choice:

Suspensions are rather more difficult, as the suspension and its resolution do not admit of a change in harmony, except in the case of a suspended diatonic seventh and its inversion [(c) below]. Very frequently the same essential note has to be repeated against the suspension and its resolution, with an auxiliary in between and a passing or subsidiary note, as may be most convenient, to complete the group (a). If the time is compound, a couple of changing notes have to be substituted for the auxiliary (b). Or the resolution may be made on a secondary harmony note (d):

Note also the following convenient idioms and their figuring:

The specimens below will, it is hoped, give a fair idea of the sort of way to work this awkward two-part combination. Some canti fermi suitable

29

SUSPENSIONS (CONTINUED)

for the purpose are provided at the end of the chapter. The result can hardly hope to be music; but the exercise gives one very helpful practice in coping with a type of situation that continually arises when two freely rhythmic parts are combined (ch. vii). As a means to that most important end, this combination will be found to justify the time and trouble expended.

Specimens:

And here are a few canti fermi specially designed for use with this section. They should be worked both as upper and (transposed) as lower parts:

Chapter Six

MIXED RHYTHM (OR FIFTH SPECIES)

A.

Fifth species is commonly stated, in text-books of counterpoint, to be a mixture of the other four. It is that, but it is also more. Other figures enter into it, and much of the bad counterpoint that is written is due to the fact that these figures are not given proper consideration. There are four of them, viz.:

(1) ♪ ♩. (2) ♩ ♫ (3) ♩. ♪ (4) ♫ ♩

or their equivalents in smaller note-values:

(1) ♫ (2) ♬ ♬ (3) ♪. ♩ (4) ♬ ♩

Of these the first, ♪ ♩. can be briefly dismissed. It is, broadly speaking,

not used in counterpoint. The rhythm is too snappy, and the reason for this, expressed in general terms, is that it infringes the contrapuntal rule which forbids a short note to be tied to one of longer value. Re-write it

thus: ♫ ♩ and its true nature immediately becomes evident.

The second figure, ♩ ♫ (or ♬ ♬), demands rather more consideration. The first note should always be regarded as an essential note. The second note may also be an essential note, involving a change of harmony, in which case the third is commonly an unaccented passing or auxiliary note [(a) and (b) below]. More rarely the third note may be a harmonic subsidiary of the second [(c) below]:

The second note may also be a passing or auxiliary note of what might be described as a semi-accented type [(d) and (e) above]. In two-part counterpoint against a C.F. in plain notes, it may always be so treated, provided (of course) that it is approached and quitted by step. Where there is a third part moving against it in free rhythm a little more caution is needed, but anyone who bears in mind the limitations generally imposed upon accented passing notes (see ch. ii), is unlikely to get into serious difficulty.

In the third figure ♩. ♪ (or ♪.♩), the dot should be regarded usually as the equivalent of a harmony note, and the odd quaver as a passing or auxiliary note (if approached by step) or a subsidiary (if approached by leap). It is only possible to treat the dot as a suspension and the odd quaver as its resolution if the latter lies a step below the dotted note. And even then the former treatment is usually preferable, for suspensions in counterpoint do not like to be hurried. (See above, p. 26.) E.g:

All of the above are correct but (d) and (f) are usually preferable to (c) and (e) respectively.

The remaining figure, ♫ ♩ (or ♫♩), is likely to impart an unseemly jerkiness to the rhythm if not properly handled. It is no bad thing for a beginner to follow Palestrina's rule and precede it by one or more short notes, especially if the second quaver (or semiquaver) in the figure is an auxiliary, as distinct from a passing note. And if the preceding note for any reason cannot be a short note, it should at any rate be no longer than a single beat note, and if in addition the last note (the crotchet) of the figure is a tied note, so much the better.

The following table of merit and demerit will serve to make clear the several points just set forth:

B.

Before trying to add a part in mixed rhythm to a C.F., the student will be well advised to practise first the shaping of a single part in the appropriate style—i.e., with suitable variety and flexibility of rhythmic pattern. All the patterns and figures heretofore described should be freely used, and the same figure should rarely or never be repeated in consecutive measures except to form a sequence. The exception, however, is an important one, for a judicious use of sequence every now and again will contribute much to the structural cohesion of the melody.

MIXED RHYTHM (OR FIFTH SPECIES)

A good plan for beginners is to take a C.F. in uniform note-values and transform it by decoration into the kind of melody described above, keeping the essential melodic contour, but altering the note-values and introducing suspensions, unessential notes, etc. according to taste. It is obviously impossible to give a detailed recipe for this procedure, but the subjoined examples, showing various possible treatments of one short C.F., will serve to illustrate what is meant. In the two more elaborate versions (B and C) the notes of the C.F. have been marked with a cross, so that the melodic relationship between the original and the variants may be seen at a glance. It will be noticed also that in (c) the mode has been changed from minor to major:

Some canti fermi of this variegated type will be found at the end of the book; the student should supplement these by decorating the plain canti fermi on pp. 51 and 52, in the manner illustrated above.

C. Once the art of writing the proper kind of melody has been mastered, it is a simple matter to add such a part above or below a given C.F. in uniform notes. Alternatively, one may first add a part in first species, and then transform it by decoration (as shown above) into the required fifth species.

Specimens:

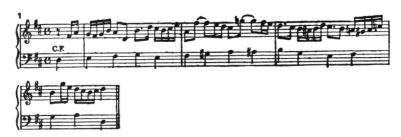

MIXED RHYTHM (OR FIFTH SPECIES)

Chapter Seven

COMBINATION OF TWO PARTS IN MIXED RHYTHM

THIS is one of the most fascinating forms of counterpoint. Success in it depends ultimately on good taste and an accurate ear. There is no rule of thumb which will ensure that the infallibly right note is put in the infallibly right place, but certain pieces of advice may be helpful:

1. The scale of note-values in both parts should correspond—e.g. if the shortest note in the C.F. is a quaver, there is no occasion for the added part to burgeon into semiquavers.

2. Something should occur on every beat—i.e. tied notes should not be employed in both parts simultaneously.

3. The parts must contrast suitably, the natural tendency being for the added part to complement the C.F. by employing short notes mainly in the places where the C.F. is deficient in them.

4. Above all, the harmonic basis must be kept clearly in view throughout, and the student must have no doubt as to whether any given note in either part is a harmony note, suspension, resolution, passing note or what not.

5. When complete, it should be a puzzle to decide, from internal evidence, which was the C.F. and which the added part. This is admittedly a counsel of perfection.

A choice of methods is available:

1. The two parts may be evolved together by a sort of spontaneous generation. This is closely akin to the process of composition; in fact, on a tiny scale, it *is* composition. This method is likely to yield the best results if done well, and the worst if done badly.

2. Recourse may be had to one of the canti fermi from Set C (p. 54), to which another part of similar character may be added. Or this added part may be written first in plain notes and then embellished in the manner exemplified on p. 33.

3. One of the plain canti fermi from Set A may first be taken and embellished according to taste. The other part may then be written direct in fifth species, or (as in method 2) written in first species and then transformed by embellishment into fifth species.

4. A part in first species may be added provisionally to a C.F. in first species, and both embellished simultaneously. And, provided the final result is satisfactory, it does not matter in the least whether the outlines of the preliminary sketch are preserved or not.

Occasional clashes may arise between an essential note in one part and a passing note in the other, or even between different unessential notes occurring simultaneously in both parts. There is no objection to such clashes within reasonable limits; but there is no rule of thumb to determine precisely what is meant by 'reasonable limits' in such a connection.

Of those given below, one or two may seem rather harsh or awkward when isolated, as here, from all context, especially if read or played slowly; but if heard in the course of an actual composition, they would scarcely be noticed.

Specimens:

Chapter Eight

THREE-PART COUNTERPOINT: NOTE AGAINST NOTE, WITH OR WITHOUT OCCASIONAL PASSING NOTES

ONCE more, each part must have its own melodic individuality, and not be a mere harmonic fill-in. The rules of melodic progression are still precisely as described in ch. i, pp. 11 and 12. The rest of the instructions there given, however, need some slight amplification, as we are now dealing harmonically with three-part chords and not merely with intervals:

1. Melodic considerations often make it advisable to leave out one note of a chord and double one of the others. If the chord is a $\frac{5}{3}$ however, the third should not be omitted, except from the first and final chords, either or both of which may be an octave-unison.

2. The third, even of a major triad, may be freely doubled, provided it is not the leading note of the key. (This exception applies not only to the principal key, but also to any subsidiary key temporarily established by modulation.) In this case, of course, the fifth has to be omitted.

3. An essentially dissonant note—the 7th, for example, in the dominant seventh and its inversions—should never be doubled, the basic reason being that its progression is not free, so that consecutive octaves or unisons must logically ensue if it is doubled.

4. From any essential 7th chord, whether dominant, diatonic, or diminished, one note has to be omitted in three-part work. The root and the seventh must both be present if the chord is to be recognizable for what it is; therefore either the third or the fifth, preferably the latter, has to be omitted.

N.B. The first inversion of a diminished triad should be regarded purely as such, not as the inversion of a 7th chord with the root left out.

5. Any $\frac{6}{4}$ chord must be identified as either a passing or a cadential $\frac{6}{4}$, and must conform to the procedure respectively indicated in the harmony books.

Specimens:

37

Chapter Nine

COMBINED COUNTERPOINT IN THREE PARTS

A. First, Second, and Third Species
B. First, Third, and Fourth Species

IT is not necessary to recapitulate, in three parts, all the mechanical processes that form the groundwork of two-part Counterpoint. But there are two special combinations, of an eminently mechanical type, which are worth practising for the sake of the technical fluency they help one to acquire. The descriptions at the head of this chapter have been borrowed, for the sake of brevity in reference, from 'strict' counterpoint. It is well that the student should know what these old terms mean; but it has been made quite clear to him in the introduction to this volume that the system of counterpoint here outlined is basically different from the so-called strict variety. The occasional use of the old terminology, therefore, should cause no misunderstanding on this point.

A. First, Second, and Third Species in Combination

Here the problem is that of adding a part in crotchets, and simultaneously another part in quavers, to a C.F. in minims. (If the C.F. is in crotchets, then of course the other parts will be in quavers and semiquavers respectively; but for the purpose of this discussion we will assume the notation to be in minims, crotchets and quavers.)

The chief difficulty lies with the part in crotchets. If this is to be a genuinely contrapuntal part, it must have a certain minimum of conjunct movement. Therefore some crotchets will have to be treated as unessential notes, accented or unaccented as the case may be. And these notes are always liable to cause harmonic confusion if the part in quavers (in which unessential notes of smaller value occur simultaneously) is not skilfully and tactfully managed.

There is one valuable safeguard against such confusion. If the quaver and the unessential crotchet are in mutual dissonance, then the quaver must behave towards the latter as though it were an *essential* crotchet—i.e. resolve correctly. In other words, the crotchet which is unessential from the point of view of the minim is essential from the point of view of the quaver. And if this secondary note of resolution (as we may term it) is dissonant with the minim, then once more, of course, it has to proceed by step:

Such dissonances are specially characteristic of Bach, who is very partial to this form of counterpoint, not usually for continuous employment, but just for an odd bar or two at a time.

It is recommended that the quaver movement should be reserved for one of the upper voices, and that the crotchet part should be completed first. The possible quaver patterns are so many and varied that it should not then be difficult to form a succession which fits the other two parts and at the same time exhibits a decent shapeliness and coherence of its own. Of the canti fermi provided on p. 51 only those in Set A should be used for this form of combined counterpoint, which is too artificial in character to be maintained without interruption for any great length of time, at any rate by the beginner.

Specimens:

B. First, Third, and Fourth Species in Combination

This is an easier combination than the last, and no special instructions are necessary, except perhaps a reminder of the sound rule (already familiar, one hopes, from harmonic study) that the resolution of a suspended dissonance should not be anticipated, except in the bass:

Once more it is recommended that the quavers should be confined to one of the upper parts, that the part in suspensions should be completed first, and that only the shorter canti fermi should be worked in this manner. And if the continuous chain of suspensions becomes too irksome and refractory, break it for an odd half-bar by substituting two untied beat notes, as shown here and there in the following specimens:

13

Students are strongly advised not to content themselves with working just a few of these two combinations. Readiness to pass on to the next chapter does not mean that these technical exercises may thenceforward safely be abandoned altogether. For any one who seriously wants to master the art of counterpoint, it is not enough to be able to do this kind of thing passably well; he must keep on practising them until they almost write themselves. Long after he has passed on to more advanced work, he should continue to work one or two of these every week, if he wishes to attain a really high standard of technical proficiency.

Chapter Ten

ADDITION OF TWO FREE PARTS TO A C.F.

A. Without Imitation
B. With Imitation

A.

If the last three chapters have been properly assimilated, this task should prove, by comparison, an easy one—easier, at any rate from a technical standpoint, than those prescribed in ch. ix, and certainly more agreeable, except perhaps for the few who find real enjoyment in the solution of purely technical problems. Nor does it call for any fresh instruction of a general nature; the guidance given in the preceding chapters should be fully sufficient.

Specimens:

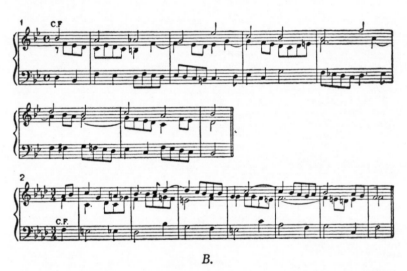

B.

Imitation is an essential feature in practically every form of applied counterpoint, such as the invention, the chorale prelude and the fugue. It is to be studied from example rather than from precept, but a few points are worth keeping in mind:

1. The figure chosen for imitative treatment should be short. It must, of course, be long enough to be recognizable as a figure, but it should not be longer.

2. It may be an independent figure, or it may be derived (by diminution) from the opening notes of the C.F.

3. The entry of the second additional part should be delayed for just so long as will enable it to make an effective answer to the first part, but not longer.

4. The figure chosen need not necessarily be maintained continuously, but it should reappear often enough for it to be perceived as a vital part of the structure. And it should participate if possible, in one voice or the other, in the formation of the final cadence. The last note of the C.F. may be prolonged for this purpose.

5. Very often an inversion of the figure will be found to fit comfortably where the figure in its original form will not. Even the first entry of the answering voice may be made, if need be, by inversion (as in the third of the examples below).

6. An occasional rest often gives point to the imitation, but such a rest should always be preceded by a beat note.

Specimens:

1. *Development of an independent figure:*

2. *Development of a figure derived from the opening of the C.F.* (in this case the figure itself is derived by inversion, but is not subsequently re-inverted in the course of the counterpoint):

3. *Development by inversion*, the figure this time being once more an independent figure:

Chapter Eleven

COMBINATION OF THREE FREE PARTS

A. Without imitation
B. With imitation

A.

As with two free parts (ch. vii), so here again the first step is the decoration of one of the plain canti fermi on p. 51. The two other parts are then added above or below, as the case may be.

An exception may be made if the C.F. is to be the middle voice. It is better in this case, in my experience, to start with the C.F. as it stands, sketch in other parts, and then elaborate the C.F. according to taste. One must, of course, bear in mind, when writing the outside parts, that the C.F. is not yet in its final stage. It must be left reasonable opportunities for decoration; if the outer parts are over-elaborated, the subsequent treatment of the C.F. may prove unduly difficult.

This method of starting in the middle may seem to us to-day to be somewhat artificial, for we have become accustomed to think upwards from a bass or downwards from a melody. But in the early days of musical composition the C.F. was always assigned to the tenor part, and in the later theory and practice of counterpoint this tradition has never entirely disappeared. One should therefore pay it a certain respect, and by so doing one does undoubtedly gain some additional insight into the nature of the contrapuntal process—which types of progression invert easily, for example, and which do not. The experience thus gained will be found invaluable on proceeding to the later study of double counterpoint and fugue.

A middle-part working is therefore given to illustrate this section of the chapter. The first example shows the C.F. in its plain form, with the outer parts added provisionally. In the second, the C.F. has reached its final stage, and the other voices, it will be seen, have been modified here and there to facilitate that process:

45

B.

As before, begin by decorating a plain C.F., but remember that the first figure presented has to persist and take predominance throughout the whole course of the counterpoint. It must reappear from time to time, therefore, in the decoration of the C.F., but not continuously, otherwise the added parts will have little or no opportunity to introduce it. It may help the beginner if a specimen working is exhibited in successive stages of progress. The C.F. used is the same as that used in the last examples: (*a*) gives it in its original shape; (*b*) shows its proposed new shape, and in addition, some sketches for the shaping of the other parts; (*c*) presents the completed result:

Just one more point. In the early stages of learning, the instruction is always given that notes are not to be repeated. This is to ensure that the beginner learns first of all to achieve that easy flowing movement which is the first essential of good counterpoint. The unskilful introduction of repeated notes causes a jolt or bump which undoubtedly mars this type of movement. But the systematic employment of repeated notes in a decorative or rhythmic figure developed methodically by imitation is on quite a different footing, and at the stage he has now reached, the pupil need have no hesitation in making use of figures like the following:

In the former of these, the second of each pair of quavers is an anticipation of the note following; it may or may not be at the same time an essential note. If it is not, it should be approached by step.

Chapter Twelve

FOUR-PART COUNTERPOINT

A. Recapitulation of Chapter VIII (addition of three parts, with or without passing notes, to a C.F.)
B. Recapitulation of Chapter IX with the addition of a fourth part.
C. Recapitulation of Chapter XI (addition of three parts, imitative or otherwise, to a C.F.)

[In four-part counterpoint, of course, it is no longer necessary to omit one note of an essential chord of the seventh. But though not necessary, it is often convenient to do so. In this case, one of the other notes has to be doubled. If the chord is a dominant or diatonic seventh, double the root. If it is a diminished seventh in root position, double the third. If it is an inversion of a diminished seventh, no note doubles conveniently, and the chord should therefore be complete. And this applies largely to the inversion even of a diatonic seventh; it is much better to have such a chord complete if possible. But remember, as has already been observed, that the inversion of a diminished triad is not to be regarded as the incomplete inversion of a chord of the seventh.]

A.

Little need be said about this. The counterpoint is basically note-against-note, but with passing notes, accented or otherwise, inserted here and there, as convenient. But there is no objection to the occasional use of tied and/or dotted notes as well, in suitable places. And parts may cross occasionally, if convenient.

Specimen:

B.

In these two varieties it is not necessary that the fourth part should be, like the C.F., in notes of uniform value. Such a part is apt to be very stiff, angular, and unmusical. It is much better that the added part should be free as to rhythm; which is not to say that it must needs be elaborate.

48

The best method of working is to complete the other parts provisionally and then add the free fourth part, after which the parts already filled in can be adjusted in detail as may be found expedient.

Here are two of the specimen workings from chapter ix, touched up here and there in this manner, with the addition of a free fourth part. The keys are different, and in the first example the C.F. has been transferred to the tenor; otherwise the two examples will be found to be substantially the same as shown on p. 39 and p. 40 respectively:

C.

To complete the course, two examples are appended in which three free parts have been added to a C.F. In the first of these, the parts are mutually independent; in the other they are unified by the employment of a single figure in the manner previously shown (see chapter x, B and chapter xi, B):

It is not within the scope of this booklet to treat of counterpoint in more than four parts, and progress within these limits can no longer be made by means of such short exercises as are here prescribed. The details already mastered will have to be applied to exercises on a larger scale, approximating more and more to free composition in the contrapuntal forms and calling the inventive and constructional faculties into play.

APPENDIX

[For general advice and suggestions on the use of the canti firmi, see the introduction, p. 9. It will probably be found that those in the treble clef are more
suitable for use as an upper part, those in the bass as the lower; but with a little
adjustment and modification all those in Set A and Set C should be found work-
able in any position.]

SET A
Major Keys

Minor Keys

SET B
Major Keys

Minor Keys

21 SET C
Major Keys

Minor Keys

Printed in Great Britain
by The Bowering Press
Plymouth